I'M A LITTLE CHOO CHOO

THIS BOOK BELONGS TO:
_____

©Copyright

By: Saffia Abdul-Haqq

Once upon a sunny day,
in a land not far away,
Lived a little train, with
colors pink and gray.

His name was Choo-Choo,
a cheerful fellow true,
With wheels that spun
and a whistle that
always blew.

Through valleys green and mountains tall, Choo-Choo chugged, delivering goods for all.

From toys to food, he carried them with care, spreading joy and laughter everywhere.

Over bridges high and rivers wide,
Choo-Choo rode with confidence and pride.

He'd chugged and puffed,
never slowing down,
Bringing smiles to faces
in every town.

Through tunnels dark and caves so deep, Choo-Choo journeyed without a peep.

With his headlamp shining bright and clear, He'd conquer every obstacle, never showing fear.

He'd transport children
to places grand,
Where castles stood in
a wondrous land.

With each adventure,
their hearts would soar,
Imaginations sparked,
forevermore.

With a toot and a hoot,
Choo-Choo would say,
"I'll be back tomorrow,
same time, same way."

For he knew his duty,
his purpose so true,
To connect the world,
through and through.

So next time you see a
train passing by,
Give a wave and a smile,
don't be shy.

For Choo-Choo's journey is never done, spreading happiness to everyone.

www.ingramcontent.com/pod-product-compliance
Lightning Source LLC
Chambersburg PA
CBHW041525070526
44585CB00002B/91